Sequoyah's Talking Leaves

Written by Mary Dodson Wade

Illustrated by Amy Bates

Sequoyah stood watching the soldiers.

The soldier who was talking had a paper.

The marks on the paper seemed to tell him
what to say.

Sequoyah had heard of such marks.

His people, the Cherokee, called them "talking leaves."

But the Cherokee had no talking leaves of their own.

They could not send messages or write stories
because their language had no writing.

That day Sequoyah had a great idea—
he wanted his people to have talking leaves, too.

Sequoyah was a young man
when he started to think about talking leaves.
He had been born in the year 1773.
As a boy, he had been very sick.
One of his legs had not grown as it should have.
He walked with a limp. But his arms were strong.
As a man, he became a silversmith.
He did fine work and made a good living.

When he married, Sequoyah built a house

for his wife, Sally.

He made her beautiful silver rings and necklaces.

Before long, they had three sons.

A few years later their little girl, Ah-yoka, was born.

Sequoyah was a busy man.

But he did not stop thinking about the talking leaves.

He decided to try writing the Cherokee language.

He began to draw pictures on pieces of tree bark—

one picture for each word.

Soon he had mounds of bark!

But this idea did not work well.

It was hard to think of pictures for words like "good."

Sally did not like her husband to waste time making pictures.

She became so angry that she burned his work.

Finally she left.

Only Ah-yoka stayed to help her father.

One day Sequoyah saw a children's book written in English. He counted the marks.

There were only 26 different ones.

Then he understood.

There was not a mark for every word.

The marks stood for sounds.

Sequoyah and Ah-yoka started again.

They listened to Cherokee people speak.

Then Sequoyah wrote down a symbol for each sound.

Soon he had 85 symbols.

At last, after twelve years of work,

he could write the Cherokee language.

At a meeting of the Cherokee chiefs,

Sequoyah and Ah-yoka showed what they had done.

The chiefs did not believe the marks would work.

"I will go outside," Sequoyah said.

"Ah-yoka will write down your words.

Then I will come back and tell you what you said."

And that is just what happened.

To show there was no trick, Ah-yoka left

and Sequoyah wrote the words.

Ah-yoka repeated them perfectly.

Then the chiefs believed.

They wanted everyone to learn to read and write.

The symbols were easy to remember.

Soon the Cherokees were writing on their houses,

on the trees, everywhere.

Before long they even had a newspaper

in their own language.

Cherokee Alphabet.

Sequoyah went to Washington, D.C.

The President of the United States

gave him a beautiful medal.

Sequoyah even had his picture painted.

But he did not stop wondering about words.

As a very old man, he went to Mexico

to learn more about languages.

No one knows where Sequoyah's grave is

or what happened to his medal.

But the Cherokees will always remember

the man who first wrote down their words.